Visualising
Vocabulary
Creative Writing
Story Settings

Preparation for 11 Plus, Independent School Exams and KS2 SATS with Practice Exercises

© B Adam 2019

1st Edition

Introduction

Creative writing is an essential skill and forms a part of many assessments and examinations. The aim of this guide is to help children ages 8-12 describe a variety of different story settings.

Visualising is key to this process. The following pages contain more than 100 colour photographs of different settings as outlined in the contents page. Each section has different pictures that highlight a different visual aspect of that topic and related vocabulary. There are a number of practise exercises at the end which provide support in helping children to describe different settings and practice using a number of literary devices and fantasy settings.

This book aims to develop strong descriptive and creative writing skills which will hopefully stand a child in good stead to produce wonderfully creative and descriptive pieces of work.

Contents

Mountains

Summit
Snow- topped peak crest apex crag slopes jagged perilous rugged

Range
Sierra imposing lofty ridge ascent descent towering picturesque

Tarn
Sapphire coloured lake pool reservoir carved

Glacier
Towering iceberg glacial ice polar cold numbing pummeling

Valley
Dale vale hollow dell dingle lush fertile

Gorge
Impassable precipitous ravine canyon gully pass chasm

Volcanoes

Active
Alive functioning spewing eject smouldering deafening exploded roared

Crater
Cavity hollow ash desolate destruction smoky rocks acrid

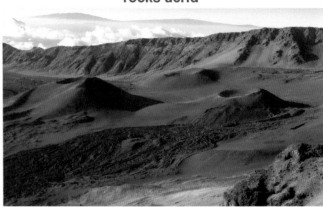

Lava
Molten fluid magma inescapable burning searing ash

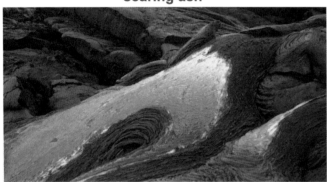

Dormant
Quiescent asleep snow topped extinct

Cloud
Venting emission discharge emit spout billowing threat

Eruption
Developing catastrophe calamity disaster cauldron clouds vapour bubbling

Caves

Mouth
Boulder strewn entrance opening jagged stumble

Stalactites and stalagmites
Slimy Tentacles pillars jagged hung rise grow glistened

Abyss
Chasm crevasse cavity void gloomy ghostly confined imprisoned

Cavern
Grotto concealed hollow tunnel uncharted explore

Labyrinth
Maze network web illuminated astray low

Subterranean
Pool glistened emerald underground concealed

Landscapes

Savanna
Grassy plains unvarying scorched arid horizon steppe

Marshland
Swamp boggy wetlands fenlands putrid decaying fetid

Moors
Uplands moorlands gust windswept heath plateau

Meadows
Field pastures rolling paddocks grassland zephyr

Arctic
Polar northern bone chilling sub zero stark uninhabited void lifeless

Oasis
Euphoria repose arid dry desert dunes scorched dusty parched bare

Cove
Bay   hidden concealed refuge inlet lagoon reef coral safety arc

Lighthouse
Beacon lofty signal silent sentinel watchtower

Coastline
Shore seaside pristine white sandy seashore island atoll archipelago

Shingle beaches
Pebbles smooth jagged crunch damp rock pools shells

Azure
Sapphire clear waters tropical sparkling ripples lapping kayak

Pier
Promenade wooden jetty pier stroll saunter tread vantage observe

Waterfalls
Cascade shower torrent gushing rapids

Torrents
Flood deluge current stream river

Meandering
Winding gentle slow paced twisting serpentine l

River bank
Edge peaceful watching embankment fringe idyllic

Reeds
Stagnant murky floating pond lake putrid

Beck
Babbling jagged stream creek brook rivulet frothed

Crimson
Leaves amber fiery autumnal crisp cascading

Orchard
Fertile yield grove harvest lush bursting

Tropical
Vegetation vines dense overgrown humid creepers muggy stifling

Canopy
Ceiling treetops sunlight overhanging rays piercing

Forest
Woodland plantation magical enchanted secret eerie emerald

Limbs
Bark gnarled bough twisted twisted knotted deformed disfigured

Creepers
Tentacles climbers vines spreading unstoppable

Bonsai
Manicured ornamental nurtured petite diminutive delicate prized

Petals
Vivid dainty beautiful lily exquisite graceful nature flora

Brambles
Thorns bush shrub berries prickly irritating clawing scratching

Fronds
Ferns leaf palm wayward overhanging sprawling verdant

Dew
Sparking adorned morning wet dripping buds glimmered

Dusk
Purple twilight nightfall eventide tinge cloudless hues

Dawn
Sunlight rays daybreak daylight piercing radiant

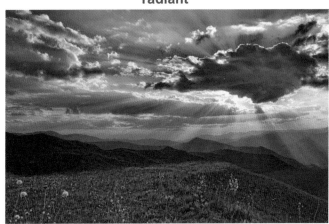

Northern lights
Flashes illumination mystical memorable atmosphere glow extraordinary

Night
Darkness celestial star adorn fathomless panoramic stellar constellations contemplate

Rainbow
Evanescent fleeting fading wisp clouds visible

Sunset
Fiery horizon skyline dipping glow gaze vivid

Lightning
Electricity forked bolt thunder spark scintillate branching

Downpour
Deluge rainstorm monsoon pour sky unexpected relentless

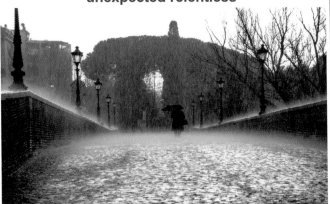

Hurricane
Tornado cyclone gale billowing obliterate debris tempest squall chaos storm

Overcast
Cloudy grey sunless dark neend dull hazy foggy rain laden

Snow
Icy blizzard avalanche shroud arctic crunching compacting

Fog
Mist haze smog dismal gloomy shadows eerie freezing silhouette

Radiant
Carefree casual relaxed sunshine sunbeams rays daisies bask

Clear skies
Vibrant fresh illuminating clear crisp

Spring
Blossom blooming thrive unfold buds burgeon

Glint
Shining glimmer dazzle lush meadows daisies abundant flourishing

Idyllic
Tranquil peaceful halcyon picturesque memorable

Clement
Mild wander venture serene delightful savour luxuriate in laze

Speed
Pace rush hurtle career tear streak whiz zoom

Overcrowded
Crammed congested overloaded heaving grimy dense

Abandoned
Graffiti wrecked neglected deserted unused unoccupied vandalised edgy

Cosmopolitan
Contemporary hordes scurry activity hive clamour bustle

Metropolis
Modern gigantic commerce prime major beneficial sprawling

Gridlock
Traffic smog tailback queue late rush fumes

Village
Coastal leisurely relaxed idyllic pristine unhurried haven

Pastures
Fields landscape countryside still nature outdoors fertile

Alpine
Fresh scenic pristine pure breeze unspoilt

Agrarian
Charming picturesque breeze traditional fresh

Rustic
Agricultural meadows homely quaint natural

Hamlet
Sleepy quiet scant sporadic settlement still

Paths and Steps

Passages
Bygone deserted gravel alley   trudge backstreet thoroughfare

Stepping stones
Jagged hidden tread leap perilous

Track
Footprints footsteps dirt course muddy

Trail
Meandering quest moors remote heath winding

Steps
Stairway jagged precarious mountainside

Cobbles
Lane market town tudor historic clip clop

Rope bridge
Rickety courage swaying rope intertwined height tread

Garden bridge
Amble walkway timber babbling stream scenic idyllic blissful serene

Suspension bridge
Arches engineering vital transportation span contemporary girders towering

Viaduct
Ancient Roman arches archway water towering stone lofty colossal strong

Footbridge
Enduring historical bygone footsteps stride

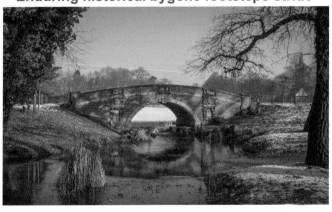

Decaying
Planks unsteady gangway dreary murky hazy

Foliage
Canopy leafage verdure emerald natural

Vandalised
Abandoned defaced echoes extended stretched grimy subterranean

Shaft
Ventilation air repair escape passage covert

Cavity
Abyss jagged limestone darkness furtive

Disused
Overgrown train tracks reverberated lurking eerie abnormal

Underpass
Winding light filled hurtle sleek engineered

Cosmos
Awestruck unrivalled galaxy constellations adorn magnificence galaxy night sky universe

Wormhole
Accelerate dimensions uncharted oblivion progress advance radiant

Eclipse
Blood coloured concealing obscure darkening prophecy omen penumbra

Orbit
Moon satellite celestial heavenly planet astonishment awe

Astronaut
Orbit space spacecraft station view Solitary resolute trepidation

Alien
Extraterrestrial colonize hospitable scour terrain

Cottage
Quaint thatched cabin chalet charming old-fashioned

Contemporary
Modern glass light- filled airy vogue futuristic

Mansion
Palatial opulent impressive breathtaking resplendent plush grand

Shack
Dilapidated dingy drab shanty disintegrating disused uninhabited deserted

Apartments
Uniform blocks balcony compact bijou

Historical
Tudor mock-tudor bygone preserved

Castle
Bastion rampart parapet barbican moat charge medieval ambush defend

Crypt
Tomb sepulchre catacomb vaut mausoleum chamber concealed sacred cursed

Haunted House
Ghostly spectre phantom shrouded dark ominous forbidding sinister

Cemetery
Burial grief omen portent lament frosty stillness spirits phantom otherworldly

Ruins
Ancient temple history epic legendary saga chronicle heroism destruction

Fortress
Bulwark barricade siege unassailable impenetrable

Features of Residential Buildings

Veranda
Porch cool airy ambience breezy relax unwind

Eaves
Lurking nestling roof gable constructed

Balcony
Relaxing sunbeams observing vantage

Threshold
Doorway formal access entrance tap thump

Hearth
Ablaze embers roaring snug homely logs welcoming

Parlour
Victorian lounge charming old wordly eccentric quirky quaint

Courtyard
Majestic spacious light open calm grand inviting exquisite

Archway
Imposing medieval embellished heavy wooden masonry portal ornate

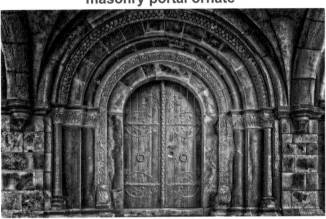

Colonnades
Limestone villa approach gallery pillars historic

vestibule
Grandiose walkway lobby murals intricate resplendent vaulted stately

Balustrade
Ornate lined stairway palatial marble

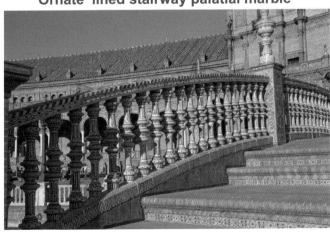

Gargoyle
Menacing lifelike fangs snarled spine- chilling sinister

Locomotive
Steam billowed chugged bygone bridge era

Marina
Port harbour luxury affluent upmarket anchored moor

Biplane
vintage altitude emit fumes engine spluttered

Sailboat
Drift wind sea ocean vessel hull helm port starboard

Tram
Trundled noisy city sightseeing jaunt excursion parade

Hot air balloon
Buoyant floating ascend soaring sky atmosphere panoramic ballast

Radiance
Coolness shining brilliant serenity attract captivate bewitch gravitate fascinate

Sparkler
Fizzed energy twinkled sparkled flash

Lantern
Antique rusty corroded clunky flickered flame flickered

Embers
Glowed cinders ash residue ashes douse smother

Conflagration
Jeopardy peril rapid fierce blazing extinguish raging

Fireworks
Colours hues burst herald festivities celebration bang erupt explode

Practice Exercises

1. Write down suitable descriptive **mountain**

vocabulary:_____

2. Write a story starter sentence using this picture.

_____

_____

1. Write down suitable descriptive **mountain**

vocabulary:_____

2. Imagine you are going to climb this mountain. Write a sentence describing your emotions

_____

_____

1. Write down suitable descriptive **volcano**

vocabulary:_____

2. Using the idea of show don't tell, write down a sentence to show that the volcano is about to erupt without actually writing that it is going to erupt.

_____

_____

1. Write down suitable descriptive **volcano**

vocabulary:_____

2. Write down a metaphor for any part of this picture.

_____

_____

1.Write down suitable descriptive **cave**

vocabulary:_____

2. Imagine you are in this cave. Write down a sentence describing what you might hear.

_____

_____

1.Write down suitable descriptive **cave**

vocabulary:_____

2. Write a sentence using a fronted adverbial to describe how someone might have ended up in this cave.

_____

_____

1.Write down suitable descriptive **landscape**

vocabulary:_____

2. Use a sentence with a hyperbole to describe this landscape.

_____

_____

1.Write down suitable **landscape**

vocabulary:_____

2. Write a sentence using alliteration to describe this landscape.

_____

_____

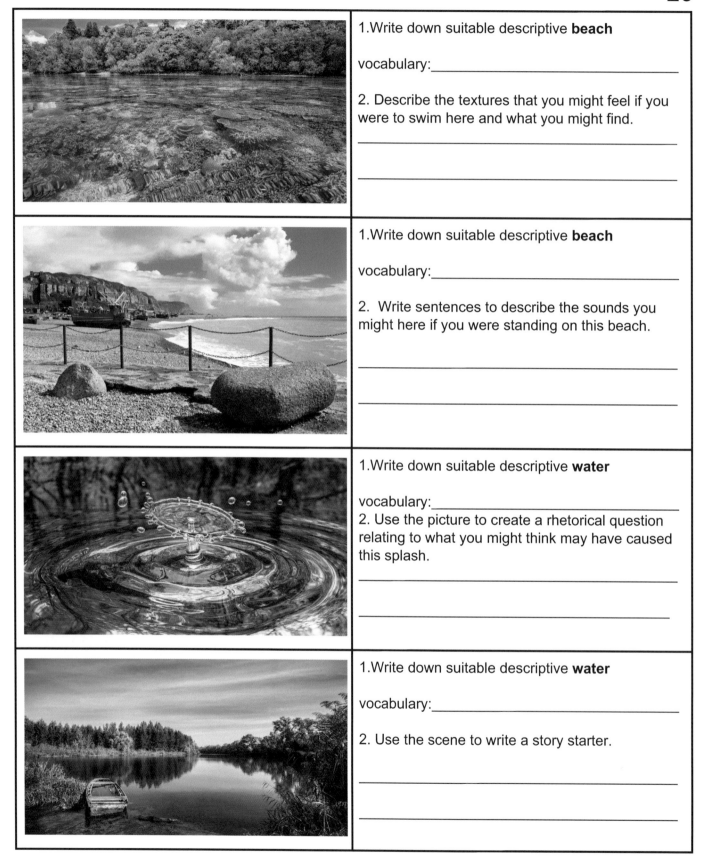

1. Write down suitable descriptive **beach**

vocabulary:_____

2. Describe the textures that you might feel if you were to swim here and what you might find.

_____

_____

1. Write down suitable descriptive **beach**

vocabulary:_____

2. Write sentences to describe the sounds you might here if you were standing on this beach.

_____

_____

1. Write down suitable descriptive **water**

vocabulary:_____
2. Use the picture to create a rhetorical question relating to what you might think may have caused this splash.

_____

_____

1. Write down suitable descriptive **water**

vocabulary:_____

2. Use the scene to write a story starter.

_____

_____

1. Write down suitable descriptive **trees**

vocabulary:_____

2. Describe the textures you can see.

_____

_____

1. Write down suitable descriptive **trees**

vocabulary:_____

2. Write a sentence to convey the different colours that you can see.

_____

_____

1. Write down suitable descriptive **plantlife**

vocabulary:_____

2. Write down a simile to describe the picture.

_____

_____

1. Write down suitable descriptive **plantlife**

vocabulary:_____

2. Describe this picture using personification by describing it with a suitable human quality.

_____

_____

1. Write down suitable descriptive **sky**

vocabulary:_____

2. Imagine you are watching this sunset. Describe how might feel.

_____

_____

1. Write down suitable descriptive **sky**

vocabulary:_____

2. Describe the colours, shades and hues in this picture.

_____

_____

1. Write down suitable descriptive **bad weather**

vocabulary:_____

2. Using show not tell, describe how the crew of the ship might be feeling in this storm.

_____

_____

1. Write down suitable descriptive **bad weather**

vocabulary:_____

3. Expand the following sentence

The _____city was struck by

_____lightning, as the _____hurricane

struck.

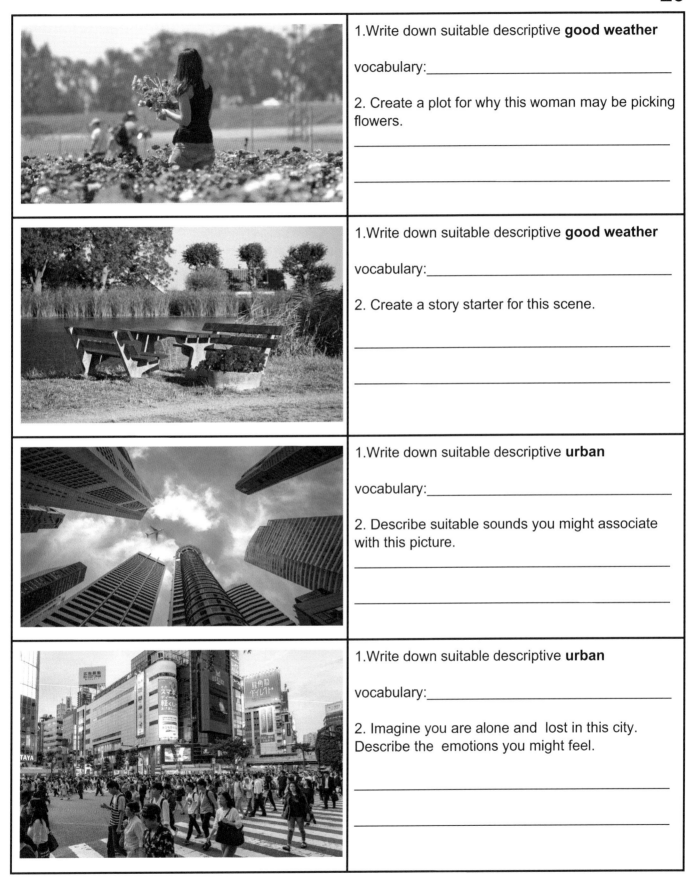

1.Write down suitable descriptive **good weather**

vocabulary:_____

2. Create a plot for why this woman may be picking flowers.

_____

_____

1.Write down suitable descriptive **good weather**

vocabulary:_____

2. Create a story starter for this scene.

_____

_____

1.Write down suitable descriptive **urban**

vocabulary:_____

2. Describe suitable sounds you might associate with this picture.

_____

_____

1.Write down suitable descriptive **urban**

vocabulary:_____

2. Imagine you are alone and lost in this city. Describe the emotions you might feel.

_____

_____

1. Write down suitable descriptive **rural**

vocabulary:_____

2. Create a dialogue for the two characters.

_____

_____

1. Write down suitable descriptive **rural**

vocabulary:_____

2. Write down what this woman might be thinking.

_____

_____

1. Write down suitable descriptive **paths and steps**

vocabulary:_____

2. Create and write a reason why someone might be at the top of these stairs.

_____

_____

1. Write down suitable descriptive **paths and steps**

vocabulary:_____

2. Write down a monologue for someone deciding which path to take.

_____

_____

1. Write down suitable descriptive **bridges**

vocabulary:_____

2. Write a dialogue between two friends deciding whether they think it's safe to cross this bridge.

_____

_____

1. Write down suitable descriptive **bridges**

vocabulary:_____

2. Using show not tell, describe something that might be lurking in the fog beyond this bridge.

_____

_____

1. Write down suitable descriptive **space**

vocabulary:_____

2. Describe this scene using a hyperbole.

_____

_____

1. Write down suitable descriptive **space**

vocabulary:_____

2. Write suitable possible plot outcomes from this scene.

_____

_____

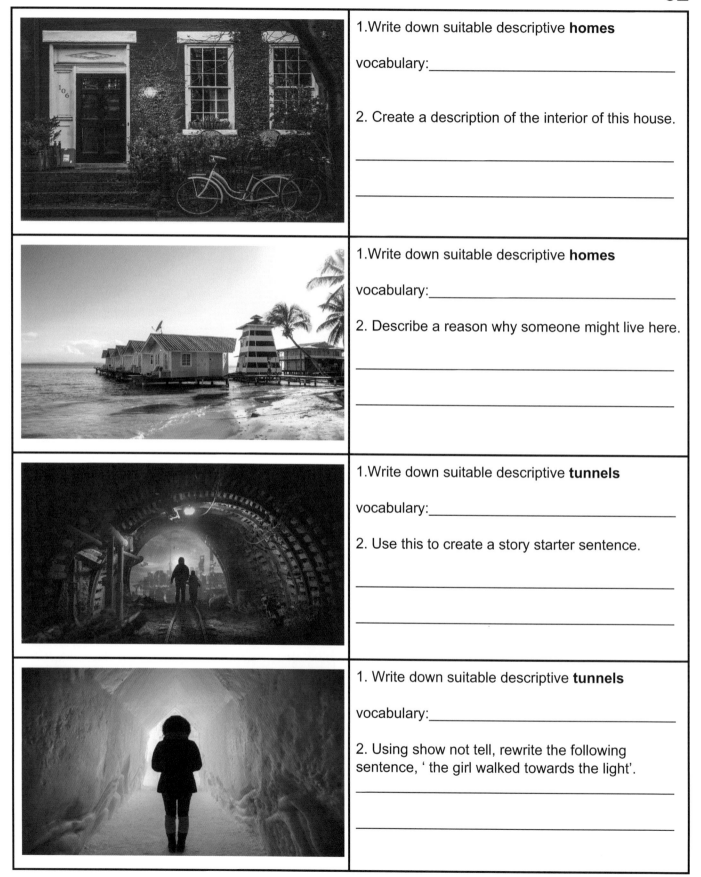

1.Write down suitable descriptive **homes**

vocabulary:_____

2. Create a description of the interior of this house.

_____

_____

1.Write down suitable descriptive **homes**

vocabulary:_____

2. Describe a reason why someone might live here.

_____

_____

1.Write down suitable descriptive **tunnels**

vocabulary:_____

2. Use this to create a story starter sentence.

_____

_____

1. Write down suitable descriptive **tunnels**

vocabulary:_____

2. Using show not tell, rewrite the following sentence, ' the girl walked towards the light'.

_____

_____

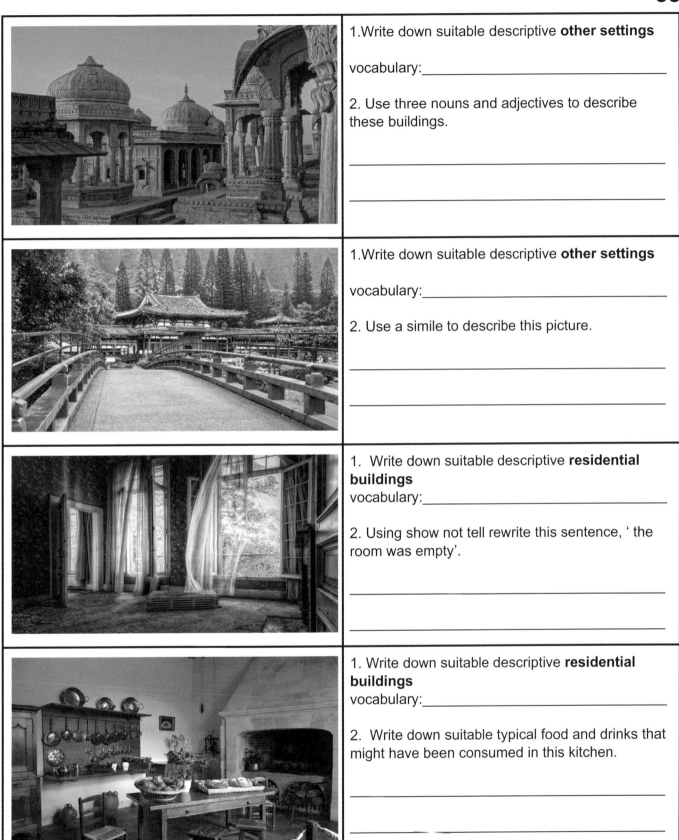

1. Write down suitable descriptive **other settings**

vocabulary:_____

2. Use three nouns and adjectives to describe these buildings.

_____

_____

1. Write down suitable descriptive **other settings**

vocabulary:_____

2. Use a simile to describe this picture.

_____

_____

1. Write down suitable descriptive **residential buildings**
vocabulary:_____

2. Using show not tell rewrite this sentence, ' the room was empty'.

_____

_____

1. Write down suitable descriptive **residential buildings**
vocabulary:_____

2. Write down suitable typical food and drinks that might have been consumed in this kitchen.

_____

_____

1. Write down suitable descriptive **historical buildings**
vocabulary:_____

2. Create a plot scene that centres around the clock.

_____

_____

1. Write down suitable descriptive **historical buildings**
vocabulary:_____

2. Write down five words related to colour and light in this picture.

_____

_____

1. Write down suitable descriptive **transport**

vocabulary:_____

2. Write three verbs and adverbs to describe this picture.

_____

_____

1. Write down suitable descriptive **transport**

vocabulary :_____

2. Use a metaphor to describe this car.

_____

_____

1. Write down suitable descriptive **fire and light**

vocabulary:_____

2. Create a plot idea for what might be in the room where these lights have been switched on.

_____

_____

1. Write down suitable descriptive **fire and light**

vocabulary:_____

2. Create an exciting plot reason for why this fire might be burning.

_____

_____

Practise Exercises for Fantasy settings

Complete the following exercises by exploring the different components of fantasy settings.

Describe the different settings in this picture.

Mountains:

Island:

Sky:

Ocean:

Fantasy element:

Describe the different settings in this picture.

City :

Sky:

River:

Bridge:

Fantasy element:

Describe the different settings in this picture.

Landscape :

Water:

Sky :

Fantasy element:

Describe the different settings in this picture.

Sky:

Landscape:

Sky :

Fantasy element:

Describe the different settings in this picture.

Cave:

Features of a Historical building:

Sky:

Fantasy element:

Describe the different settings in this picture.

Trees:

Landscape:

Good Weather:

Features of a home:

Fantasy element:

Describe the different settings in this picture.

Space:

Sky:

Landscape:

Fantasy element:

BIG	IMPORTANT	SERIOUS	BREAK	CRY
Colossal	Main	Significant	Shatter	Weep
Enormous	Chief	Momentous	Smash	Lament
Gigantic	Principal	Grave	Crack	Sob
Vast	Key	Urgent	Snap	Wail
Massive	Major	Crucial	Fracture	Snivel
Immense	Critical	Vital	Fragment	Bawl
Huge	Prime	Pressing	Splinter	Blub
Gigantic	Eminent	Weighty	Disintegrate	Whimper

CUT	EAT	FAT	GOOD	GOOD
Gash	Consume	Plump	Fine	Righteous
Slash	Devour	Stout	Superior	Moral
Lacerate	Ingest	Overweight	Excellent	Principled
Slit	Wolf down	Heavy	Outstanding	Honourable
Pierce	Chew	Flabby	Splendid	Scrupulous
Puncture	Munch	Broad	Wonderful	Trustworthy
Penetrate	Chomp	Podgy	Tremendous	Commendable
Score	Swallow	Chubby	Awesome	Admirable

HAPPY	HIT	LAUGH	LOOK	MOVE
Contented	Strike	Guffaw	Glance	Advance
Cheerful	Slap	Chortle	Gaze	Proceed
Merry	Pound	Roar	Gape	Progress
Jovial	Smash	Howl	Peer	Budge
Jocular	Wallop	Chuckle	Scan	Stir
Carefree	Whack	Giggle	Focus	Shift
Buoyant	Hammer	Snigger	Glimpse	Bolt
Radiant	Pummel	Titter	Gawp	Tears
Euphoric	Thrash	Cackle	Observe	Sprint

NICE	OLD	SAY	SAY	SAY
Enjoyable	Elderly	Speak	Interrupt	Retort
Pleasant	Mature	Utter	Articulate	Babble
Agreeable	Aged	Declare	Query	Chatter
Delightful	Senior	State	Converse	Prattle
Satisfying	Ancient	Announce	Answer	Croak
Lovely	Venerable	Remark	Reply	Hiss
Marvellous	Bygone	Assert	Mumble	Communicate
Good	Former	Avow	Whisper	Affirm

SHORT	SMALL	THIN	WALK	WALK
Small	Little	Narrow	Stroll	March
Teeny	Small Scale	Fine	Amble	Trek
Tiny	Mini	Lean	Saunter	Wander
Miniscule	Bijou	Paper thin	Hike	Ramble
Teeny	Diminutive	Scrawny	Trudge	Roam
Low	Pint sized	Skinny	Stride	Traipse
Stubby	Measly	Scraggy	Patrol	Lurch
Miniature	Cramped	Emaciated	Prowl	Stagger

Printed in Great Britain
by Amazon